THE PINNACLE OF MY LIFE

BY BEN MATICH

authorHOUSE®

AuthorHouse™
1663 Liberty Drive
Bloomington, IN 47403
www.authorhouse.com
Phone: 1-800-839-8640

First published by AuthorHouse 3/9/2011

ISBN: 978-1-4567-4715-2 (sc)

Printed in the United States of America

*

<u>I DEDICATE THIS BOOK</u>
<u>TO MY RELIGION…</u>

TABLE OF CONTENTS

*

<u>INTRODUCTION</u>

Greetings, to all of my readers; out there. Welcome back, to our forum; this is my "<u>FOURTH</u>" book.

I wrote this one, because due to what happened to me, I have hit a rather weird part; of my existence.

On a certain day, things which had been so horrible, from the past, seemed to finally, be turning around; for the better.

I could not believe it! (Stuff was improving). Plus, I was going to be more positive, at that; too? (Noooo), it couldn't be, but yes; it was true.

I had found a purpose, a couple of new goals, and I even had balance, from which; I'd be able to focus by.

Like so many, I had thought to myself, at least now, I have not only my reason to live- from

(God), which was publishing my books; but I also have the payoff as well.

I could now physically see, touch, and believe in (Something)- and (Someone) again, totally turning away, from both (Beth), and (Tina)- with respect; but then it happened!

Worse then the bomb, that (June) had laid forth- unto me, was this; my plan totally backfired!

(Shelly) took the idea, of (Her and Me), actually being a notion, to consider- then twisted it, like a wet towel, and yanked cruelly; with a SNAP!!!

She did this, as hard as, she possibly could- and since, (I) am a (Half-Ghost); I began to flicker.

After I had been stunned, I had no choice, but to leave- for (She) had created, no alternative routes, of satisfaction, and unfortunately, (She) also succeeded in; rejecting all of mine.

(Shelly) may say, it was neither one, of (Our) faults- (She) might even say, it was (Me) perhaps, but (I) say, it was (Her); who had clunked (Us), and\or, what could; have been.

This, is where, I would also mention- that because (Shelly) is gone, I am sad, hurt, lost, and totally back, to being nothing again; just (Me) and (My Religion).

I believe (They) now concede…

By Ben Matich

<u>PLEASE FORGIVE ME</u>

Hi (Jill). How are you? I hope you don't hate. I know that when we spoke, and finalized, it did not go; all that great.

Admired to the end, indeed yes, you were, but also, you had been involved; and I didn't want to be the cause of a "Spur".

I certainly understood why, when (Me), and (LTC) laughed- (You) were in, no position, to join us, or even, take (Me) up; on such a chance.

Now, it should be, quite clear, to you, (Friend Jill)- why (I) couldn't push, it's because, I did not wish, to get beat up, or turned into; a slop of moosh.

Although I am, really glad for you, I can assure, that as I wish- all the best, to (Your) way, I fastened, the seal, of (It's) crest: upon the down-low…

By Ben Matich

THE BEE

I was once, wandering along, in a meadow, I cared about nothing- just a peaceful ray, (I) was; all made up of gentle.

I encountered flowers everywhere, in the lovely clean grass- so as I looked around, I then stated; 'Ah Alas'!

I picked one up, though there were many, and I decided; to call it (Penny).

Woe be to me, as I gave in a smell, (Bzztttt)! I felt pain, on my nose, and screamed; 'Oh Hell'!

I dropped my flower, and said, 'I don't like you anymore!' The flower looked up, and said, "It's not me pal, look over there, it was that; little gal!"

I looked where the flower had hinted, angrily as now, I squinted- and sure enough, I did see! [A circling, and buzzing around; Bumble Bee]!

I shouted, 'Hey yo-yo! You stang my nose, and now I say, you shall have to go'! The Bumble Bee looked back at me, and asked, "Who do you think you are"?

I chased it furiously, on no uncertain terms, the retched insect flew and flew- until I captured it, the (Creature's Fate), would soon now become over, "Satisfactorily" to me.

The Bumble Bee, then asked, "If I surprise you, then will you let me go?" I thought for a moment, and then answered, 'Yes, it shall be so'.

As I released it from my hands, the Bumble Bee asked, "Can you guess my name"? I could not, so I claimed, 'No'.

It then said, "Nickki", and just like in reality, when she moved away, on that terrible day; I realized I just had to let her go…

By Ben Matich

THE BEE: 2

Traveling distances, had always seemed to me, to be a "Way out There", kind of concept, that is; until I lost someone close.

A very dear friend, this person was, who I may never get back, and due to this loss- I did have, a panic attack, of course, I had told my friend, that it would all; be ok though.

I had seen this before, but I never have, wanted to see; it again. I say, these torrid haunts, unto me, befall the worst of memories, (such as not being able to forget Laura); yet I do try to learn from "their" consistence.

Strange, that a simple shift to (Melanie), can boil me up, but I "<u>DID</u>" - wish to part our paths amicably, yet the truth was, I did not set well with it; however.

Even a jerk like me, wants to at least "<u>SEEM</u>",

strong in the eyes; of a (Beauty Girl). Right guys? Even when, I really wasn't; all that.

Whenever the (Summer Time) approaches, I always go off wildly, because I do not like-all the bugs, especially the spiders; and bees. (Yuckkk)!!!

Nothing makes much sense to me, these days; at all. People we care about die, (Life) pretty much is unpleasant, and here I am- trying to be straight, the whole time; feel me?

[I do know this]:

I can say, adamantly here, when (Nickki) left, there was nothing, I could do, but when it gets down to (Melanie's), departure from my life- it was my fault, for she was a "Good Girl", and I am just not that "Nice Guy", anymore, (for I don't want to be, ever again); not with anyone.

[I just can't]…

By Ben Matich

*

THE BEE: 3

I never really liked, bugs that much, for I was always afraid, that me; they would touch.

It is true, I am an ex- exterminator, but I just couldn't do it, as a professional; career-wise.

The bug thing, of too much insects in your life, can really get at a guy; trust me.

Probably like the (Army), might be, a little bit too much, for some; at a certain point. Same here, I guess; in a way.

Here is a story towards this: One day, I had seen a Wasp, hovering over a thorn bush, and I watched, as it quickly thereafter; landed on it.

I also had seen a Bumble Bee, a little farther, but still relatively close by; Me and the Wasp. It was doing the thing, where they just creepily buzz around; on the ground.

There was, the Bumble Bee, acting as if it were, a shark- preparing for something; like it's lunch.

I screamed, 'You won't dare come near! Get out of here! For between Me, and this Wasp, all you can do, is stay far, and with fear inside yourself; gasp!'

The Bumble Bee, looked right back at me, and said, "I will insult once for your egotistical head, then fly away, before you make for me; my bed".

'Oh please, I retorted, nothing that you say, could bother me; in any type of way!'

It then spoke, "Nickki". I was baffled, as it flew away, because I contemplated, what that name meant to me- remembering when Nickki, had moved on, and I was once more; unhappy.

Word to the (L.O.B.), that I was before, because even to this day, some things- I suppose, just can not, be forgotten, and that also, would include; certain people...

By Ben Matich

*

TEARS OF MY SORROW: B'S VERSION

Like so many, I had lots of friends, but they eventually; all had moved away. (Darn Oh Darn)! Those great neighbors; that just don't ever stay!

I guess, I must have, teased too much, and made an (Over-Amount) of fun; or something.

[It can not possibly, just be, as simple; as life goes on].

I have to be at fault somehow, (Shelly) might declare, but I still (Loved) her, so other blondes; please be well aware.

No flirting for me, though denied was (B); I guess I earned that too.

When (Melanie) came into the picture, it was a really bad time, I'd say easily, to her credit; the (Little Doo).

[Both (Shelly), and (Melanie), are my "Gems",
I do indeed; contend].

I know, I was mean, but (JR), is still lingering,
around in my thoughts daily-though she seems, to
not even know, that I still care for her, consequently
as, "Politics", had taken (Me) out; of her boat.

I've earned all the misery somehow, that I have
obtained, I just don't know how; or why.

'What does the Lord have to gain'?

[I'm curious; says I].

You would think, (God) would be sympathetic,
but as it turns out, when it's going to be, all about
(Me); (He) simply prefers my cry...

By Ben Matich

*

THE APOLOGY THAT COULDN'T BE GIVEN

To (His Demise), I see he left, we could not curb, that small and little cleft- by which upon, had been indented, all because of a secret thought, that (I) had; basically presented.

Fools could see, that (Her) and (Me), were made of nothing, for (His Daughter) could not set things up- like those (Gardening Women), for they'd be hearing; (Sarcastic's) verbal thrashings.

The (Roddened Weasel), had bore witness; to such a crazed moment!

I say, 'Wait'! (Weasel meets Snowman)? What a strange "Trite" this is! I'm amaaazzzeeeddd!!!

In any event, one looming, the other in a tree; and what about (JTDK)?

These friends of mine, were lost, because of a "Yoga Type", plus I had said; a strange word.

Either way, I must say, I still miss, (Dream Girl's Ann)- though motioned to (Elizabeth), yes) I did; and (Oh Alas)!

[I do also, (Say-Yay), towards the later; turned years].

Even with (Nickki), though at some points, my fault; it will still be NO!!!

By Ben Matich

*

<u>CONCLUSION</u>

As my readers, pat themselves on their backs, I say; (Good Job)! You made through, another one; of my books!

[Ho-Hum-Dee-Dol-Dee-Dum].

(Yes)! This is tremendous! (I know).

So, until the next time, we meet again; I say this:

Life is never easy. Things are always changing, and if you are an (Old-School) type of character, like I am, you sure feel similar, to the (Dinosaurs); from way back when.

That's right! I say, (We, The Ancient History, Of Mind Set), are totally, in my opinion, that is; PREHISTORIC!!!!!

[I hate it]!!!!

Nothing can, be done though, for it is- how the world seems, to operate, and (I) just end up being, a (Blue Punk); in all of it's function's.

I try to adjust, figure it out by (Myself), and to listen to (Shelly's) advice, (Mel's) too; but it's hopeless.

[Right before they each left me, I admit]:

That for whatever (Moronic, Ridiculously Stupid, Confounded, Corny) reasons, (I) can summon up; it's all too obvious.

[I IGNORED THEM]...

By Ben Matich

*

BONUS: "QUOTES"

<u>FAVORITE PHRASES\QUOTES THAT THIS AUTHOR BELIEVES IN WHOLEHEARTEDLY, AND TRIES TO LIVE BY; EACH DAY:</u>

"I may be stupid, but I'm not dumb".

"Anyway now so, and then, there there; and then then."

"Sanford style, rumbolee rumbolee; rum rum rum".

"Bazoo, bazoo bazee, bazoo; ba zoo zoo zoo zee zee".

(Finally), me and one of my, very best friends, would fool around, all of the time, with this one; (WOLF MAN CALL):

"Yaaahh, Woo-Woo; WOOoOOOO"!!!!

Anyone who knows us, can tell you, pathetically towards my regard, at least, that yes; it happened.

(Laughs)…

By Ben Matich

*

OTHER BOOKS BY THIS AUTHOR

-)Heavenly Struck
-)Heavenly Struck (Vol. 2)
-)Golden Treacherys

~These books are available to buy at "Author House". You can call (1-888-519-5121); to order them.

~Heavenly Struck (Vol. 2), and ~(Golden Treacherys), are also available to buy; at "Amazon. Com", your local bookstores, and "Abebooks. Com".

~If you can't find them, ask your stores; if you can order them.

(Thanks).